Seasonings!

Devotional Poetry

by

Florence Glister

MOORLEY'S Print & Publishing

© Copyright 2006

All rights reserved. No part of this publication may be
reproduced, stored in a retrieval system, or
transmitted, in any form or by any means,
electronic, mechanical, photocopying, recording
or otherwise, without the prior
written permission of the publishers.

There is no restriction on the public reading of the poems
providing the copyright restrictions as
set out above are adhered to.

British Library Cataloguing in Publication Data.
A catalogue record for this book is available
from the British Library.

ISBN 0 86071 592 2

MOORLEY'S Print & Publishing
23 Park Rd., Ilkeston, Derbys DE7 5DA
Tel/Fax: (0115) 932 0643

An introduction from the author:-

I was born in a small Norfolk village and have lived in the same area all my life. The wonder and beauty of the world around me, and the changing seasons, have always given me so much joy and pleasure. I have tried to express this in the poems I have written, giving all the praise and glory to God, the Great Creator "He has done all things well". I pray that this book will be a blessing to those who read it and that God's Name may be honoured and glorified.

Springtime

The flowers of Spring are beautiful,
They bring us so much cheer
Telling us Winter days are gone
And Summer is drawing near;
The snowdrop is the first to appear,
So pure and clean and white,
No trace of earthly stain is seen
As it pushes its way to the light.

The crocus quickly follows
In purple, white and gold,
A carpet of these beneath the trees
Is a real joy to behold;
But nothing is more beautiful
Than a carpet of purest gold
The wonderful colour of daffodils
As their petals so bright unfold.

Tulips in many colours,
And dainty primroses in bloom,
All quickly appear to say Summer is near,
Away with darkness and gloom.

The trees are clothed so splendidly
In many shades of green
And we wonder again at the beauty
Of Springtime's peaceful scene.

As each new Springtime comes around,
Let us remember anew
That the hand of our God created it all,
Green grass and skies so blue;
Let's thank Him for each lovely thing
Which every day is new
For baby chicks and ducklings,
For kittens and puppies too.
But most of all let's thank Him
That He gave His Son for us
That we might be made clean and new,
Clothed in His righteousness;
He died that we may have new life,
That we might be forgiven,
And even the glory of Springtime fades
When compared with the glory of Heaven.

The Glory of Springtime
The beauty of Spring is all around,
New life in all we see,
Flowers come bravely through the ground
Whatever the weather may be.

Snowdrops lift their pure white heads
Just tipped with pastel green,
So delicate, we wonder how
They keep so pure and clean.

Daffodils so bright and fair,
Quiver and dance in the breeze,
Golden yellow, so beautiful,
Like a carpet under the trees.

Then the primrose comes, such a dainty shade,
With perfume sweet and rare,
With crocuses and violets,
They spring up everywhere.

Tulips of many colours and shades,
Red, pink, yellow and white
Spread beauty all around us,
A truly wonderful sight.

The leaves on the trees are fresh and clean,
So many shades of green,
I wish I could paint pictures
Or capture it all on screen.

Our Father, the Creator God,
Gives us so much to enjoy,
Trees, flowers, birds and sunsets,
The ever-changing sky.

With so much beauty all around
We lift our hearts and sing
In praise and worship to our God
For all the joys of Spring.

Good Friday (1)

How wonderful the love of God
That He could give His only Son
To die upon that cross of shame
For all the evil we have done;
He died that we might be forgiven;
He bore the burden of our sin,
That we might know the love of God
And have His peace and joy within.

No one can plumb the depths of pain
That He endured to set us free,
The crown of thorns, our sin and shame,
All this was borne so patiently.
And looking up to God in Heaven
This prayer was said for me and you,
"Forgive them oh My Father,
For they know not what they do".

The cross on which the Saviour died
Was planed from wood His hands had made.
He made the rocks that formed the tomb
In which His lifeless body lay;
All things in earth and heaven were His
And yet He laid them all aside
On that Good Friday long ago
When He for us was crucified.

But oh the joy that fills our hearts
To know that this was not the end
For He has triumphed over death
And on this fact we can depend;
On that third day He rose again,
The one who for us bled and died
Now lives, all glory to His name,
And we by faith are justified.

We have His peace within our hearts,
We know His presence day by day
And as we journey on life's road,
He will go with us all the way;
Until one day we see His face,
Once marred for us on Calvary's tree,
I want to glorify His name,
Because I know He died for me.

✝ ✝ ✝

Good Friday (2)

This is the day we remember
How Jesus was crucified,
How on that cruel cross of shame
For us He bled and died.

Bearing the sin of all mankind,
Though spotless and pure was He,
On Calvary's hill He paid the price
To set the whole world free.

As they hammered the nails into His dear hands,
He looked to His Father above,
And prayed that He would forgive them,
Can we comprehend such love?

'Twas the love that He had for you and me
That led Him to suffer and die,
So that all our sin might be blotted out,
On that cross He was lifted high.

'Good Friday' is for you and me,
But for Him 'twas an awful day,
And it's right that we should remember
The price He had to pay.

When He bore the burden of all our sin,
The Father's will was done,
That we might be reconciled to God,
He gave His only Son.

He gave His life that we might live
With Him eternally,
I'll praise His name and worship Him
– For He gave Himself for me.

The Risen Lord

'Christ is Risen', such glad tidings,
Send them forth from shore to shore,
'Christ is Risen', Hallelujah,
Let us worship and adore;
Calvary's Cross stands stark and empty,
Empty also is the tomb,
Christ has triumphed, death is vanquished,
Scattering all our fear and gloom.

'Christ is Risen', what a message,
How it thrills our hearts anew,
For His death and resurrection brings
Such hope to me and you;
One glad day we will be with Him,
'Twas for us He bled and died,
That our sins might be forgiven,
That we might be justified.

He is reigning now in Heaven,
Seated at His Father's side,
All His pain and suffering ended,
There forever glorified;
We rejoice and sing with gladness,
Let's repeat it o'er and o'er,
'Jesus Christ the Lord is Risen',
And He lives for evermore.
Hallelujah!

Easter Joy

Oh the joy of Easter morning,
Jesus Christ the Lord is Risen
He has triumphed, death is vanquished,
Let all praise to Him be given.

All the pain of crucifixion
On that cruel cross of shame,
He endured to bring salvation
That forgiveness we might claim.

God's own Son so pure and holy,
Bore the burden of our sin
That we might know His forgiveness,
That we might have peace within.

Oh the joy of knowing Jesus
As our Saviour, Lord and friend,
This will cheer in days of sadness,
Life in Christ can know no end.

New life surging all around us,
Flowers that bloom and birds that sing,
All unite each Spring to tell us,
Christ is Risen, Christ is King.

May the glorious Easter message
Fill our hearts with joy once more,
Jesus Christ the Lord is Risen,
Let us worship and adore.

Easter Praise

On this happy Easter morning
How our hearts rejoice and sing
Bringing all our praise and worship
To our Risen Lord and King.

Jesus Christ the Lord is Risen,
He endured the cross and shame,
Over death He rose victorious,
Let us praise His Holy Name.

As He walked earth's changing pathway,
Tasting all its joy and pain,
He did much to ease life's burdens
As He lived with sinful men.

He had power to cast out demons,
Heal the sick and ease their pain,
And when hearts with grief were stricken,
Raised their dead to life again.

He so loved He died to save us,
Shed for us His precious blood,
On that cruel cross He suffered,
Making there our peace with God.

In the tomb they laid His body,
For three days it rested there,
Then He rose again victorious,
That we might His glory share.

So rejoice for Christ is Risen,
Let us worship and adore,
He has triumphed, Hallelujah!
And He lives forever more.

It's Easter Day

Oh wonderful joy, it's Easter Day, Jesus the Lord is Risen;
He has conquered death, no more to die,
He is living and reigning now on high,
And we worship the Risen Lord.

On that cruel cross of Calvary, sin's penalty was paid;
He gave His life that we all might live,
He was raised from death new life to give,
And we worship the Risen Lord.

O Lord as we worship You today, You give us joy and peace;
We just want to say we love You Lord,
We are trusting in Your Precious Blood,
And in You our dear Risen Lord.

The Joy of the Easter Message

The disciples were sad as they came to the tomb,
At the dawn of that first Easter Day;
For Jesus, their Lord had been crucified,
And His body taken away.
A stone had been laid at the mouth of the tomb,
But this had been rolled away;
When they stooped and looked in, the body had gone;
Only the grave clothes remained.
Two men stood by them in shining white robes,
And to their amazement said,
"Why seek ye the living here at the tomb?
He is Risen, just as He said."

Mary Magdelene also came to the tomb,
Very early, before it was light,
And as she stood weeping, she looked for her Lord,
But saw there two angels in white.
"Woman, why are you weeping?" they asked.
"My Lord has gone," she replied.
"Please tell me where you have laid Him,
The One who was crucified."
Then she turned around and saw Jesus,
But knew not that it was Him,
She thought Him to be the gardener,
Were her eyes with tears made dim?
He said just one word: "Mary",
And she recognised her Lord,
The One who died had Risen again,
Her Saviour and her God.

Two others journeying homeward
On the Emmaus road,
Were speaking of all that had happened
To make them feel so sad;
When Jesus came and joined them,
They didn't know it was Him
He asked them why they were so sad
As He walked along with them.
They told Him how the Saviour
Had been crucified and slain,
How all their hopes were shattered,
Their hearts were filled with pain.
But now, some say they've seen Him,
Should any doubt remain?
For He said when He was with us
That He would rise again.
They asked the Stranger to come in,
For it was late they said,
Then they recognised the Saviour

As with them He broke the bread.
How their heartbeats must have quickened,
Filled with wonder and delight,
Their eyes were opened, and they knew Him,
then he vanished from their sight.

Many others also saw Him,
Can we doubt what they have said?
Jesus Christ the Lord has risen,
He has triumphed over death.
We His children also witness,
In His life we share a part,
Praise the Saviour, Hallelujah!
For He lives within our hearts.

So with this glad Easter message
Thrilling all our hearts today,
Jesus Christ the Lord *is* risen,
Gladly we our homage pay.
He is reigning now in glory,
Let us worship and adore,
Jesus lives, the Mighty Conqueror,
And He lives for evermore!

Easter Day

As Easter morning dawns once more,
We praise our Risen Lord
For He has triumphed over death,
Fulfilling His own Word
Though sinful men had done their worst
And nailed Him to the tree
He rose triumphant from the grave
From death to set us free.

The cruel nails, the crown of thorns,
The hatred and the scorn
The awful pain and mocking,
For us He bore it all.
The weight of all our sin and shame
Was laid upon Him there
That we might have eternal life
And in His glory share.

When redemption's work was finished,
They laid Him in the tomb
They set a watch and sealed it,
With an enormous stone.
But only three days later
That stone just rolled away
As our Saviour rose victorious
At the dawn of Easter Day.

He first appeared to Mary,
Then to many others too
That they might spread the joyful news,
Knowing that it was true.
Their Master really was alive,
Had risen from the tomb
And by His Resurrection
Scattered all their fear and gloom.

Each Spring as new life comes afresh
To all the earth around
It speaks to us of how in Christ
New hopes and joys are found.
Because He triumphed over death,
New life to us to bring
We lift our hearts to worship Him,
Our Risen Lord and King.

His Finished Work

On Calvary's cruel cross of shame,
The Saviour died for you and me
'Twas there He shed His precious blood,
From sin and death to set us free;
The crown of thorns, the cruel nails,
That pierced His blessed hands and feet,
The soldier's sword thrust in His side,
The sacrifice for us complete.

No tongue or pen can ever tell,
Just what it cost for Him to bear
The awful burden of our sin
Laid on His sinless spirit there;
The Father's face was turned away,
He could not look upon Him there,
His only Son made sin for us,
That we His Holiness might share.

No other could for sin atone,
But on that day the price was paid,
Redemption's work for us was done,
His body in the tomb was laid;
For just three days it rested there
And then came Resurrection power,
My Saviour triumphed over death,
And now He lives forever more.

One day He'll come again to earth
To claim the bride for whom He died,
We know not when that day will be,
But we shall see Him glorified;
The head that wore that crown of thorns
will wear a crown of glory bright
And we will share His glory there,
Where all is peace and joy and light.

He Knows and Cares

When you're worried and perplexed
Or are feeling really vexed,
God will hear you when you pray
He will help you through each day.

When our days are filled with joy
Happy songs our hearts employ,
Easy then it is to bring
Praise and worship to our King.

When your heart with grief is torn
And a loved one's death you mourn,
Do not seek to hide your tears
Jesus knows and really cares.

He came down to earth from heaven
Showing us the Father's love,
On the cross He died to save us
His is love all loves above.

So whatever life may bring us
Joy or sorrow, pain or fear,
We can know His peace and blessing
We are safe within His care.

Summer Delights

Oh how I love summertime,
The long bright golden days,
To sit beneath a leafy tree,
Enjoying its welcome shade;
The birds they sing so sweetly,
Or are busy finding food,
Keep really still and watch them,
It will do you so much good.

The sky so often deepest blue
With fluffy snow-white clouds
And breezes blowing gently,
Cast shade patterns all around;
The garden at its very best,
With colours clear and bright,
Each tiny flower so perfect,
Giving pleasure and delight.

The scent of roses fills the air,
There's honeysuckle too,
Also carnations, pinks and stocks,
To name but just a few;
The evening hours are best of all
To enjoy their perfume sweet,
A gentle stroll amongst the flowers
Just makes the day complete.

At times we find the days too hot,
Or there's a long dry spell
Then we are glad to have the rain
Refreshing all so well;

We breathe the air so pure and clean
After a gentle shower
In thunder rolls and lightning's flash,
We sense God's mighty power.

We have so many blessings,
So much beauty all around
How we should praise and thank the Lord,
For the gifts of sight and sound;
For birds and flowers, trees and grass,
And every living thing,
To God the Great Creator,
Our grateful thanks we bring.

Summer

Summer is a golden time,
With sunshine warm and bright
So many lovely things to do to fill us with delight;
Visits to the seaside, picnics on the shore,
Holidays and outings, and special treats galore.

Fields of golden sun-ripe corn wave gently in the breeze
When days are hot there's welcome shade,
And coolness 'neath the trees;
It's good to stop and rest a while, enjoying every day
The magic hours of Summer, for too soon they flee away.

Summer flowers are beautiful,
Their perfume rich and rare,
Carnations, Roses, Lilies, Stocks, we find them everywhere;
Petunias and Marigolds, their colours bright and fair,
Fuchsias and Hydrangeas and others we hold dear.

Lush green meadows are ablaze
With Buttercups and Daisies
And many other little flowers grow in unusual places;
But if we had no sunshine or gentle showers of rain
None of these good things would grow in garden or on plain.

The birds sing sweetly in the trees, they're busy all day long,
They often cheer our spirits
With the sweetness of their song;
As in the early morning dawn's chorus we can hear
We lift our hearts in praise to God, and thank Him for His care.

Our loving Heavenly Father gives us all things to enjoy
His creation is so wonderful it fills my heart with joy;
For all His good and precious gifts sent freely from above
Let's thank and praise our Father God
For Summer's gifts of love.

Seaside Musings

How good it is to sit by the sea
On a lovely sunny day
To watch the waves roll gently in,
Without a hint of spray;
The gulls float gently on the waves,
They look so peaceful there
At the slightest sign of danger,
They rise swiftly in the air.

The children playing on the beach,
Building castles grand
Making tunnels, turrets and moats,
So skilfully from sand;
They search for coloured pebbles and shells,
Some common and others rare,
Decorating their castles,
The flags fly proudly there.

Patient Dads make sand pies
For tots and toddlers small
It gives them endless pleasure,
There are shouts of glee from all;

Mum then takes them paddling,
At first they're not too sure
But soon, as the tiny waves tickle their toes,
They lose all trace of fear.

I've pictured such a peaceful scene
With everything calm and bright,
But stormy seas and crashing waves
Can be an awesome sight;
In gale and tempest, storm and flood,
Our earnest prayer should be
That our God who rules the elements
Would care for all at sea.

We read so often of Jesus
Being on or near the sea,
He taught from a boat, and prepared a meal
On the shore of Galilee;
He also walked on water
And the storm obeyed His will,
Even so, whether life be stormy or calm,
He whispers His 'Peace be still'.

A Rainy Day

One day the rain was falling fast
The outlook dull and dreary,
It made me think of saddened hearts
Of folk by pain made weary.
How often do I pray for those
Bowed down by sin and sorrow?
Who needs the Lord's uplifting power,
His help today, tomorrow.

But rain brings us God's blessings too
Without it nothing grows;
Our crops would fail and pastures die

As every farmer knows.
Then let us try to thankful be
When rain comes splashing down,
Our Father knows just what we need
So let us smile – not frown.

We know the sun will shine again
Above the clouds it's there,
And soon its welcome rays will come
Our hearts to warm and cheer.
Then let us always praise the Lord
In sunshine or in rain,
He ever pours His blessings down
And His love remains the same.

The Changing Skies

Have you watched the sky on a sunny day
When clouds are fluffy and light,
They drift along in the gentle breeze,
A truly wonderful sight.

When rain is falling the sky is grey,
No break in the clouds we may see,
But we know the bright sky is still above,
Though hidden from sight it may be.

When a storm is raging the clouds are dark,
Split by lightning dazzling and bright,
Then a rainbow appears with colours so clear
And the darkness is turned to light.

When the day is dying, and the sky is aflame
With sunset's wonderful glow,
No artist can fully capture the hue
That our glorious sunsets show.

At night the stars shine in the sky,
A sky of deepest blue,
The moon sheds abroad its silvery light,
And lends enchantment too.

Our lives are like the changing skies,
Some days are happy and glad,
But storm clouds gather and tears may fall,
And our hearts are heavy and sad.

Yet our Father's care is always there,
Like a canopy above,
To cheer our hearts and comfort us,
With His unfailing love.
He is with us on our darkest days,
He shares both our joy and sorrow,
And whispers to our troubled hearts,
'Just trust Me for tomorrow'.

So as we view the sky above,
Be it cloudy or bright and fair,
We know God's love is over all
And we're safe in His loving care.

Our Thanksgiving Prayer (1)

Once more we want to thank you Lord
For every token of Your love
For Harvest safely gathered in,
Such blessings all Your goodness prove;
We thank You for the golden grain
That goes to make our daily bread
For fruit and vegetables and flowers,
For beauty all around us spread.

For families and friends and homes,
We want to thank You Lord today,
For every good and precious thing
You give to cheer us on our way;
For all the beauty of the earth,
The splendour of the sky above,
And for the greatest gift of all,
We thank You Father for Your love.

We think of those in other lands
Where there is famine, want and war,
Where many people starve and die,
Where water is not clean and pure;
It makes us realise afresh
How much dear Lord we owe to You,
How much we have to praise You for,
Your love and care in all You do.

We ask You Lord to bless these gifts
Which we have brought our love to show,
Just use them for Your Glory Lord,
That others of your love may know;
We pray for all who are in need
And just commit them to Your care,
Please show us Lord how we can help,
And how we can our blessings share.

And so we bring our thanks and praise,
For life and health, for joy and peace,
For every blessing found in Christ
Whose boundless love will never cease;
Help us to always thankful be
For every blessing on life's way,
As we rejoice and praise you Lord
On this our own Thanksgiving Day.

Thanksgiving Day

Once more it's our Thanksgiving Day and as we look around
We praise God for all the blessings that in our land abound;
He cares for all our many needs, provides our daily bread,
How often do we thank the Lord, say 'Our God is Good'?

The food we eat, the air we breathe, rain falling from above,
The golden sunshine warm and bright are all tokens of His love;
We have so much to thank Him for - homes, families and friends -
If we wrote down all our blessings the list would never end.

For a good harvest gathered in we bring our thanks today,
And for all the many blessings showered on us on life's way;
Help us always to be thankful for Your love and tender care,
That we may not be selfish but all our blessings share.

For there are others in this world oppressed by famine sore,
By floods and earthquakes, war and hate, and some are really poor;
They have no homes in which to live, so little food to eat,
We just ask the Lord to help them, their many needs to meet.

And so we bring our gifts of love on this Thanksgiving Day,
Praying that God will bless them and speed them on their way,
To bring some comfort and relief to those who are in need,
And in our giving we will find we too are blessed indeed.

And for the greatest gift of all, Jesus, God's only Son,
We bring our grateful thanks and praise to Him the Holy One;
He'll satisfy our deepest needs and keep us in His love,
Till we gather at that Harvest Feast in our Father's house above.

For one day He will take us to that home so bright and fair,
Where war and want shall be no more, we will His glory share,
We can trust the future to Him as with grateful hearts we bring
All our love, and praise and worship to our Saviour, Lord and King.

A Thanksgiving Prayer

Today we've gathered in this church
To thank and praise You Lord
For Your many gifts of Harvest time,
Your love to us out-poured.
Our every need has been supplied
By Your own loving hand,
How blest we are to live and work
In such a favoured land.

In many countries there has been
So little food to eat,
Because of earthquakes, floods and war,
Folk dying in the street;
We've seen the pictures on TV
And how our hearts have bled,
Oh Father in your mercy
Provide their daily bread.

We bring our gifts to You today
And ask that You will bless
And use them to meet special needs,
Some weary souls refresh;
Help us to always thankful be

For all Your love and care
To pray for those who are in need,
And all our blessings share.

We thank You most of all for Him,
Who left His home above
Who came to earth to die for us,
To show us Your great love;
Accept our thanks in His dear Name
On this our special day
Bring many more to trust in Him,
The Life, the Truth, the Way.

You satisfy our deepest needs,
You give us joy and peace,
We know the love You have for us
Will never, never cease;
So on this our Thanksgiving Day
we praise Your Holy name
And thank You Lord for Harvest time
And every blessing given.

Our Thanksgiving Prayer (2)

Once more we want to thank You Lord
For all your loving care,
For the way you have watched over us
Throughout another year;
We think of all the blessings showered on us day by day
Oh give us grateful, thankful hearts,
For this dear Lord we pray.

We take so much for granted
In this our favoured land
Just help us to remember
All comes from Your loving hand;

We do our part, prepare the ground, and seeds of promise sow,
   It's only by Your grace and power
   They germinate and grow.

We thank You for the harvest Lord
   Now safely gathered in,
   For fields of golden sunripe corn
   And every blessing given;
For fruit and vegetables and flowers, for beauty all around
   We lift our hearts in praise to You
   In whom all good is found.

We bring our harvest gifts to You,
   All tokens of Your care
   To ask that You will bless them now,
   As we with others share;
And pray for all who are in need, the hungry, sick and poor
   That You will meet their many needs
   From Your own boundless store.

We also long for them to know
   The greatness of Your love,
   In sending down Your only Son
   From His own home above;
To die on Calvary's cruel cross that we might be forgiven
   That whosoever will may come
   To be with Him in Heaven.

Dear Lord on this Thanksgiving Day
   We lift our hearts in praise
   Help us trust and honour You
   In all our future ways;
To show the love of Jesus as we live for You each day
   Be with us Lord and bless us now,
   In His dear name, we pray.
      Amen

Garden Musings

When sitting in the garden on a bright and sunny day
The birds they sing so sweetly
And flowers bloom in bright array;
I'm rejoicing in the sunshine, in the breeze and leafy shade,
And in all the many wondrous things
Our Father's hand has made.

The birds teach us a lesson as they sing a joyous song,
If we counted all our blessings
We would praise Him all day long;
The flowers are decked in splendour, every colour, every hue,
And he whose hands created all,
He careth for us too.

There is so much to tell us of His greatness and His love,
As we view the beauty of the earth
And of the sky above;
A garden is a place of rest until we see the weeds,
Some small, some great, but all
Have grown from very tiny seeds.

And as weeds spoil our garden, even so sin spoils our lives,
Every weed must be uprooted
Or it seeds and multiplies;
All our sins must be forgiven, cleaned by Jesus' precious blood,
If we'd reach our full potential
In the garden of our God.

The Holy Spirit's love and power will beautify and bless,
As we open up our lives to Him,
His loveliness express;
In the glory of the garden our hearts rejoice and sing,
And we bring our praise and worship
To our Saviour, Lord and King.

The Great Creator

When I look around this wonderful world that
Our God the Creator has made,
My heart thrills with joy and I just give Him thanks
For the wonders around me displayed.

He gives us the trees with their welcoming shade,
All differing in leaf and design,
In autumn He clothes them with colours so bright,
No artist His work can outshine.

The beauty of flowers no words can describe,
How they cheer us and gladden our way:
All were created by His loving hand,
For us to enjoy day by day.

The birds singing sweetly give us such joy,
Their plumage just shines in the sun;
And not even a sparrow falls to the ground but He knows,
For He care for each one.

The grandeur of mountains, the hills and the dales,
Great rivers, the sea and the land;
The blue of the sky, and sunsets so bright,
All show the great powers of God's hand.

There are many more wonders of which I could tell,
Of animals fierce, great and small;
The pets that we have that bring us such joy,
Our great God created them all.

He has given us all of these things to enjoy,
But the greatest of all gifts He gave,
When Jesus His Son came from heaven above,
That we by His death might be saved.

Salvation He offers to you and to me,
But we the decision must make,
Whether we accept or reject His great gift,
This is the step we must take.

God gave His all when He gave His dear Son,
To suffer and die in my place,
I just want to thank Him and give Him my all,
A sinner saved by His grace.

Harvest Thanks

For all God's many gifts of love
Throughout another year
We bring our grateful thanks and praise
For His great love and care;
We pray 'Give us our daily bread',
But He gives us much more
He satisfies our every need
From His own boundless store.

For all the joys of Harvest time,
For fields of golden grain
For fruit and vegetables and flowers
We praise God's Holy Name;
The beauty of the earth around,
The blue of skies above
The autumn tints, and sunsets bright,
All these reflect His love.

We bring to God our Harvest gifts
To show in some small way
Our gratitude for that great love
Surrounding us each day.
And as our hearts by love are touched
So let us gladly share
With those in need around us,
Just show them that we care.

We also want to share with them
The message of God's love
How he allowed His only Son
To leave His home above;
To die for us on Calvary's tree
That we might be forgiven
Made pure and clean that we one day
Could be with Him in Heaven.
Till then let's strive to do our part
To care for those in need
To share with them the Bread of Life,
Their hungry souls to feed;
Let's praise and thank our Father God
Who reigns in Heaven above
For friends and homes and Harvest time,
And all His gifts of love.

A Harvest Prayer

We have come to thank You Lord today
For Your great love and care
For all the good things we've enjoyed throughout another year,
You have blessed us in so many ways
And given once again
A Harvest rich and plentiful of fruits and golden grain.

We take so much for granted
As we plan our meals each day
Such a wonderful variety of foods are on display,
We never need be hungry Lord,
There is always something good
To make an appetising meal of real nutritious food.

But there are others Lord we know
For whom things have been bad,
Disease has ravished many farms and made us feel so sad,
Fewer cattle, sheep or lambs,

Graze on their dales and hills
Farmers' livelihoods have gone and hearts with pain are filled.

Others have been flooded out,
Their homes and cropped fields too
There are so many other needs, we bring them Lord to You,
You've been so very good to us,
Help us to do our part
To care for needy people, and to comfort aching hearts.

Now many hearts are torn with grief,
By sorrow pain and loss,
We ask You Lord to comfort them and draw them to the cross
That in the Saviour they may find
Your healing and Your peace
May put their faith and trust in Him whose love will never cease.

Accept the gifts we've brought today,
Just bless and use them Lord,
May they speak to others of Your love, Your true and faithful word,
As on this our Thanksgiving Day
We thank You once again,
And for each token of Your love we praise and bless Your Name.

Harvest Thanksgiving

For all your many gifts of love we bring our thanks today,
For your great faithfulness of Lord, your care along life's way;
The many blessings we enjoy, the harvest gathered in,
The sun and rain, and gentle breeze, all have by You been given.

We have so much to thank you for but many are in need,
Who have no food or water Lord, for them your help we plead;
We think of those who have no home, no family or friends,
No place to sleep, no church, no school, the sad list never ends.

We pray for all whose lives are torn by sorrow and distress,
We bring our gifts and ask that you some needy ones will bless
And let your blessing rest on all who seek your love to show,
And by Your Spirit and Your power bring many Your love to know.

But we on this special day have simply gathered here
To thank You for the harvest Lord, for all Your love and care;
For we can only sow the seed, we then depend on you
To make it germinate and grow and yield a harvest true.

And for the greatest of all gifts, Jesus, your own dear Son
Who died for us on Calvary's cross for all the wrong we've done;
We bring You all our thanks and praise as at Your feet we fall
Accept our worship and our love, for you are Lord of all.

So on this our Thanksgiving Day we just say 'Thank You, Lord'
For such a bounteous harvest, and for Jesus the Living Word;
He truly is the Lord of Life, who died and rose again,
Let us faithfully sow and nurture the seed until He comes to reign.

Our Harvest Prayer

This is our Thanksgiving Day, to You dear Lord we bring
Our grateful thanks for all Your love and care in everything;
Once more the harvest gathered in has filled our hearts with praise
As well as rain and cloudy skies You gave us sunny days.

You know dear Lord just what we need, Your promises are sure,
Seed time and harvest, day and night from age to age endure;
You've given us so many things, choice vegetables and fruit,
The golden corn provides our bread, from beet comes sugar sweet.

But Lord we pray for those today who know what hunger is,
Nothing to give their children Lord, it should not be like this;
So many things have happened Lord to bring such pain and grief,
Oh may we from our hearts respond to bring to them relief.

Help us not only Lord to pray but from our plenty give
That they may have the things they need, to eat, to drink, to live.
But most of all we want them Lord to know of Your great love
In sending Jesus Christ Your Son to earth from heaven above.

He came that we might know You Lord, to show how much You care
For all the needy people, all around us, everywhere;
He came on Calvary's cross to die that we might be forgiven
That one day we might gather at Your harvest feast in heaven.

And so we bring our harvest gifts for You to bless and use
To help and cheer some needy folk, whoever You may choose;
That they may come to know You Lord, to trust Your love and care,
To praise and magnify Your name, this is our harvest prayer.
Amen

Autumn

Autumn is so colourful it really cheers our hearts
With its splash of brilliant colours before the winter starts;
We gaze in awe and wonder as nature decks the trees
With leaves of scarlet, gold and brown, the artist's eye to please.

Hedgerows too in autumn dress are such a splendid sight
With blackberries and rose hips and hawthorn's berries bright;
Maple leaves are golden before they gently fall
Such beauty thrills us as we sing, "The Lord God made them all".

Chrysanthemums in the garden can be autumn's favourite flower
Their rich and vibrant colours are all we can desire.
Abundant fruits and berries are now on shrubs and trees
There's a beauty all around us still and fragrance in the breeze.

Swallows and migrating birds to warmer climates fly
As sunsets really wonderful paint the western sky;
We notice now that daylight fades earlier every day
And many things remind us winter is not far away.

Autumn can be chilly but there's much to warm our hearts
As we praise God for His goodness, the blessings He imparts;
Let us go on to know Him in fuller, deeper ways
To be drawn much closer to Him as we reach our Autumn days.

Autumn Glory

Soon Autumn tints will deck the trees and hedgerows everywhere,
Scarlet berries, coloured leaves, they bring us so much cheer;
Trees all clothed in splendour - red, yellow, brown and gold
Our hearts just overflow with joy as such beauty we behold.

Chrysanthemums and Dahlias in many glorious shades
Make a really splendid show, their colours slow to fade;
Then there's Michaelmas Daisies and sprays of Golden Rod
We view with wonder all these things created by our God.

In gardens fruits are ripening - rosy apples, mellow pears,
Such bountiful provision by a God who really cares;
Harvest has been gathered in; fields are brown and bare,
But soon a carpet of rich green will spring up everywhere.

Sunsets really beautiful paint the western sky
With colours oh so startling to dazzle every eye;
How glad I am that I have eyes to see these glorious sights,
I ache for those whose eyes are blind, who can't tell dark from light.

Each evening as the sun goes down just close your eyes and pray
Say, "Thank You Lord for colour, for the beauty of each day";
Then as the night sky deepens from pale to darkest blue
Commit the night once more to God – He will take care of you.

When the night is over, dawn's colours flood the sky
Rosy pinks and turquoise, pale yellows to enjoy;
The sun appears in splendour and the earth is bathed in light,
Then all the glory of God's world, once more bursts on our sight.

Autumn Days

Autumn colours are wonderful, the hedgerows all ablaze
With scarlet berries, leaves of gold and every other shade;
Trees are really beautiful, clothed in colours bright
A walk in the woods on a sunny day will fill you with delight.

The fallen leaves beneath the trees make a carpet soft to the tread
And as the leaves drift gently down, the birds fly overhead;
Autumn flowers are gracious in their robes of red and gold
And in many other colours much beauty we behold.

Japanese Anemones nod their fragile heads
Chrysanthemums and Dahlias now deck the flowerbeds;
Summer flowers have faded; their beauty now is past,
Daylight hours grow shorter, twilight approaches fast.

The dawning of a new day has a beauty rich and rare,
As dewdrops sparkle on the grass there's a freshness everywhere;
The glory of a sunset no tongue or pen can tell
The One who made the universe, He has done all things well.

Let's thank the Lord for colour, for the blue of skies above,
For all our many blessings, for His greatest gift of love,
And let's just thank Him once again for the precious gift of sight
Which allows us to see colour and makes our pathway bright.

Winter

What can I say of winter days, so often dark and cold?
Yet even then there's beauty as we watch each day unfold;
When sunlight glistens through the trees that stand so straight and tall
Quite leafless now, but lovely still, showing their grace to all.

The birds come to us glad to feed on all the scraps we save
They slowly learn to trust us and really are quite brave;
We buy them bags of peanuts and tasty sunflower seeds
To help them through the coldest days; to satisfy their needs.

When hoar frost decks the hedgerows and trees with dainty lace
We see the handiwork of God, its beauty and its grace;
No human hand could ever work such an intricate design
It really is so wonderful that such a God is mine.

When snowflakes drift so gently down to clothe the world in white
It speaks to us of purity, God's holiness so bright;
Reminding us of how His Son died on that cruel tree
That we might be made pure and clean, from sin's stain to be free.

There is something so enjoyable about a winter's day
When work and school is over and we take our homeward way;
We draw the curtains early to shut out the cold dark night
And thank God for His gifts to us of warmth and love and light.

So even on a winter's day just lift your voice and sing
In praise and thanks to God above for every precious thing;
For the joys of love and fellowship that cheer us on our way
And all the many blessings that come with each new day.

Thoughts on a Snowy Day

As I looked out on a blanket of snow
So pure and dazzling white,
It made me think of God's Holiness,
His great purity so bright.

As the sun shone down on this sparkling scene
My eyes could not take the strain;
And no man can look on God's Holiness
If the taint of sin remains.

But the pure white snow was soon sullied and spoiled
And its dazzling whiteness gone;
Nothing could make it clean again
And it melts in the warmth of the sun.

I think again of God's Holy Word
Its message so clear and plain;
Though our sins are many and scarlet now
We can be made white again.

Yes, whiter than snow, what a wonderful thought
Made white by the precious blood,
The Saviour shed on Calvary's cross
To bring us back to God.

So as you look at the snowflake so pure
Drifting softly and gently down,
Just thank the Lord for the cleansing power
Of Jesus – His own dear Son.

Christmas

Christmas is such a wonderful time
When we hear from friends old and new,
Cards and letters come through the door,
Bringing greetings warm and true.

The gifts that we give, and those we receive,
All wrapped with such thought and care,
Show the love of family and friends
And those we hold most dear.

The Christmas Tree decked in splendour and light
Is beautiful .to see,
And the wreath on the door just welcomes us in
As one big family,

But all of these things would mean nothing to us
If God had not sent His Son
To be born as a baby in Bethlehem
On that first glad Christmas morn.

The cards with their message of peace and goodwill
Just point to the King of Peace;
And the love that's wrapped up in the gift of God's Son
Gives us joy that never will cease.

The carols we sing have just one glad theme;
This is the message they bring,
We tell it afresh "Rejoice and be glad,
Come worship our Saviour and King".

Christmas Peace

It's Christmas again and with gladness we bring
Our praise and our worship to Jesus our King
The angels appeared to the shepherds at night
They were amazed and just trembled with fright.
But the angel said "Fear not, glad tidings we bring,
A Saviour is born", then the heavenly host sing:
"All glory to God and His peace be on earth,
Goodwill to all men, regardless of birth."

We too should rejoice for a Saviour is born
We remember His birthday each glad Christmas morn;
Let's praise Him and thank Him for all His great love,
For leaving the glories of Heaven above,
To come to that stable, a dear baby small,
Then later to die to bring peace to us all.
May that peace fill our hearts as we go on our way
Thrilled by His coming that first Christmas Day.

The Christmas Gift

What does Christmas mean to you?
Is it just presents and fun?
Or do you also remember the day
God gave to the world His Son?

The greatest of gifts came to Bethlehem
And was born in a stable bare,
For no room could be found for this Holy Child
And Joseph sought shelter there.

Is there room in your hearts and home for Him?
Have you welcomed the Christ Child in?
For He is the gift the Father gave
To save us from our sin.

This Christmas as you open your gifts,
Remember the Father's love
In sending to us His only Son
From the glory of Heaven above.

Remember it was for you and me
He travelled that weary road
From Bethlehem to Calvary
This precious gift from God.

Then let us join with the angel throng
In praise to our God above
And say "Thank You dear Lord Jesus"
For that gift whose name is Love.

Christmas Joy

We celebrate gladly our dear Saviour's birth;
For He left Heaven's glory and came to the earth
To be born as a baby at Bethlehem's Inn;
His cradle a manger where cattle had been.

The shepherds were watching their flocks in the field,
When a bright light from heaven the angels revealed:
"Fear not," was their message, "A Saviour is born,"
So we can be happy this glad Christmas morn.

The Wise Men from eastern lands sought for a king;
The star led them onward, their treasures to bring.
And kneeling before Him in wonder and awe,
They gave to Him gold, frankincense and myrrh.

His name is called Jesus, this dear, holy child,
Born to a virgin so gentle and kind,
And Joseph was chosen to shelter and care
For Mary and Jesus, so special and dear.

This baby grew up, He was sinless and pure;
No other could claim to have kept all God's law.
He then gave Himself to die for our sin,
That we might be cleansed and have His peace within.

The message of Christmas is peace upon earth;
The Saviour has come, we rejoice at His birth.
And so with the angels we carol and sing
All glory to Jesus, our Saviour and King.

What gifts can we bring Him who came from above,
That first Christmas morning to show us God's love?
Our hearts and our lives are all we can bring
As we worship before Him our glorious King.

Christmas Thoughts

At that first Christmas long ago
The Saviour came to earth below,
Not to a palace or costly hall,
But to a lowly cattle stall.

Joseph, with Mary in need of care,
Was glad to find rest and shelter there,
And in that stable on Christmas morn,
Jesus, the Light of the World was born.

Although He was a Heavenly King,
He left His home in glory bright
And came to this poor world of sin
On that first starry Christmas night.

To Him the lowly Shepherds came,
They kneel before Him and adore,
The Wise Men brought their costly gifts
Of gold and frankincense and myrrh.
The gifts He brings to you and me

Can never deck a Christmas tree.
More costly far than any gem,
Only His blood could purchase them.

It was for us the Saviour came,
His death can be our only claim.
To make us fit to be in heaven,
Knowing through Him we are forgiven.

From Bethlehem's Inn to Calvary's hill,
He went, God's purpose to fulfil.
From cattle stall to a cross of shame,
For me He journeyed, praise His Name.
He gives us pardon, joy and peace;
His love for us will never cease.
Let's praise and bless the Lord of all
Who graced that lowly cattle stall.

Christmas

Christmas has come with all of the joys
Dear to the hearts of girls and boys.
Many presents and lots of fun
From early morn till day is done.

The presents we give are all chosen with care
As we wrap up each one we just whisper a prayer,
"May your Christmas be happy, enriched by God's love,
As daily His goodness and mercy you prove."

The Christmas tree there in its own splendour stands
Trimmed with such careful, loving hands,
With tinsel and stars and baubles to bright
All enhanced by switching on twinkling lights.

We remember afresh how our Saviour was born
In that humble stable on Christmas morn,
God's gift to the world to show us His love
Sent down from the glory of Heaven above.

This precious gift was His only Son,
Jesus our Lord, the Holy One,
He came to this world to suffer and die
On Calvary's cross to be lifted high.

No longer a baby at Bethlehem's Inn
He came to redeem us and save us from sin.
Today let us worship and thank Him anew
For His wonderful love for me and you.

We Worship Him

We worship Him, who came to earth
From heaven above, to a lowly birth.
His cradle was a cattle stall,
And He was just a baby small.

We worship Him, who came to tell,
Of God's love for sinful men,
And He has broken the power of sin,
That we might be brought back to Him.

We worship Him, who healed the sick,
Made lame men walk, the dumb to speak,
Who told us of His Father's love,
Of a home prepared for us above.

We worship Him, who on that tree,
Suffered such pain and agony.
That we might have our sins forgiven,
And be made fit to go to heaven.

We worship Him, who rose again,
No more to suffer death or pain.
He now is at the Father's side,
Risen, Ascended and Glorified.

We worship Him, who one glad day,
Will call us from this world away,
To be with Him in glory bright,
Where all is love, and joy, and light.

So gladly then we'll praise His name,
Tell others of His love for them.
That they may turn from all their sin,
And join with us to worship Him.

The Christmas Message

It's Christmas time and we rejoice for Jesus has been born,
And Christians throughout the world salute this happy morn.
He left His Father's home on high and came to earth below,
To show us that God loves us and that we His love might know.

The Shepherds keeping careful watch over their flock that night
Were startled by a brilliant light and a shining angel bright;
"Fear not," the angel said to them, "To you is born this day
A Saviour who is Christ the Lord." He then went on to say
"All glory be to God on high; peace and goodwill on earth;"
We also sing and joybells ring rememb'ring Jesus' birth.

The Wise Men travelled from the east to greet the new-born King.
Gold and frankincense and myrrh, these are the gifts they bring.
A bright star shining in the sky had led them safely there;
They kneel before Him and adore this kingly child so dear.
We give our gifts at Christmas time to those we know and love;
What can we give the Saviour who for us came from above?

He longs to have our hearts, our love, unworthy though we be;
He will receive us if we come, He died to set us free;
From Bethlehem's poor manger to Calvary's cruel tree,
He journeyed through this world of sin for love of you and me.
Let's bring Him all our thanks and praise as at His feet we fall
And worship Him the new-born King, Saviour and Lord of all.

The First Christmas Day

As Christmas once again draws near,
Our hearts are filled with joy,
Remembering the Saviour's birth,
And how for us He came to earth,
On that first Christmas Day.

The gifts we give remind us all
God gave His Son for us,
It was the greatest gift of all,
But we gave Him a cattle stall,
On that first Christmas Day.

How hard it must have been
To come to this dark world below,
To leave His home in glory bright
Where all was peace and joy and light,
On that first Christmas Day.

The Shepherds and the Wise Men came,
With joy they worshipped Him,
They recognised the Promised One,
Veiled in flesh, God's only Son.
Born on Christmas Day.

Then let us join the angel throng
To worship and adore
The One who came from Heaven above,
To show to us our Father's love
That first glad Christmas Day.

So gladly we our carols sing
And worship Him, the newborn King,
Rememb'ring why He came to earth,
We celebrate our Saviour's birth,
On this glad Christmas Day.

The Old Year (1)

Christmas is behind us, the New Year on before
The Old Year almost ended, what memories do we store?
We think of all God's goodness, how His love He has outpoured
He has helped us and watched over us, our true and faithful Lord.

He gave comfort in our sorrows, stood with us in our pain
And when our days were filled with joy,
He was with us just the same;
For His love it never changes, He just blesses us each day
We never need feel lonely, He goes with us all the way.

We can leave the future to Him, He knows what lies ahead,
If we put our hand in His hand, there's no need for fear or dread;
If we trust Him as our Saviour and crown Him Sovereign Lord
He will never, never leave us, He is faithful to His Word.

So step out into the New Year, in His strength and power be bold,
Whatever you may say or do you cannot change the old;
But you can strive, God helping you, to make the coming year
Much better than the old one, just trust His love and care.

The Old Year (2)

We thank God for another year,
For all His wondrous love and care,
He has been with us all the way,
Guiding and keeping us each day.

He has supplied our every need;
He is a faithful God indeed;
No other friend stays by our side,
Our every stop and step to guide.

He's filled each day throughout the year
With love we can with others share,
He wants our love for Him to show
As more like Him we seek to grow.

"Do not fear for I am with you",
God's own word to me and you,
And I know what e'er befalls us
His great love will see us through.

In days of pain and deep distress
We've proved His care and faithfulness;
He comforted in sorrow's hour,
And in our weakness showed His power.

When happiness and joy were ours
He shared with us those golden hours,
So let us praise His Holy Name,
"Jesus, for evermore the same".

As we look back we thank the Lord
For giving us His Holy Word,
To guide and keep us day by day,
Walking with Him along life's way.

On Jesus now we fix our gaze
And give Him all our future days,
That we may for His glory live,
To Him all praise and honour give.

The New Year (1)

It's the middle of Winter, the weather is cold,
As we welcome the New Year,
Say farewell to the Old;
With all of its joys, its mistakes and its sorrows,
Put firmly behind us
We look to the morrow.

A New Year is special, we all need to ask
For the Lord to be with us,
To help with each task;
As we seek His guidance and blessing each day,
We know He is with us
Each step of the way.

A happy New Year is one that is spent,
Trusting the Saviour
And being content
With all of the wonderful blessings He gives,
As deep in our hearts
We rejoice that He lives.

We don't know the future or what it will bring,
But His grace is sufficient,
He knows everything;
He goes on before us
Preparing the way to draw closer
To Him every day.

Though trials, troubles and testings may come,
We can lean on His strength
We are never alone;
As each day unfolds we are safe in His care,
And He whispers "My child
There is no need to fear".

So once more this New Year dear Father we pray,
That You will just guide us
And show us the way,
To appreciate always Your blessings and love,
Make us ready to meet You
In glory above.

The New Year (2)

A New Year lies before us
And our resolve should be
To walk more closely with the Lord,
To serve Him faithfully;
He has promised to be with us,
He will keep us in His care,
So as we journey onward
Let us trust and never fear.

He will guide us daily,
Step by step along life's way,
We will feel His presence near us,
He will hear us when we pray;
He'll be with us when we're happy,
Comfort us when we are sad,
What a Friend we have in Jesus,
Loving Saviour, Precious Lord.

Let us now surrender to Him
Every day of this New Year,
Ask forgiveness for our failings
As we come to Him in prayer;
By His Spirit He will help us,
Give us power to conquer sin,
And, the greatest of all blessings,
We will know His peace within.
Peace that comes through trusting Jesus,

For He shed His Precious Blood
That our sins might be forgiven,
That we might have peace with God:
Peace that passes understanding,
Peace because the price is paid,
On this New Year ask His blessing,
Then go forward unafraid.

The New Year (3)

Another New Year unfolding, what does the future hold?
None of us knows the answer no matter what we're told.
To some it may bring sadness, to others happiness,
What lies in store for each of us we would not dare to guess.

But God our Heavenly Father knows, and we can trust His power
To meet every situation, even in our darkest hour,
If we cast our cares upon Him we can fully trust His love
He will fill our hearts with His own peace as we His goodness prove.

If our days are filled with gladness, He will share this with us too
Let's remember to include Him then in all we plan to do,
We know He is a faithful God and with confidence we say
He will never, never leave us, He'll go with us all the way.

So let's commit this New Year to Him, whatever it may bring
Relying on His faithfulness and love in everything,
May He bless, guide and keep us, trusting in His power and love,
Till by His grace, we see His face and worship Him above.

He Cares for You

One day I'd been madly rushing
To fit in so many things,
Thinking only of life's turmoils,
Wishing that my feet had wings.
Sinking down so spent and weary,
'Neath a green and shady tree,
Two birds twittering together,
Seemed to bring these thoughts to me.

Said the Robin to the Sparrow,
"I should really like to know
Why these anxious human beings
Rush about and worry so.
They've no time to sing God's praises,
Little time to spend in prayer,
On their faces they wear daily
Such a look of anxious care."

For a moment they were silent,
Then they sang a merry song,
Sparrow thought he'd found the answer,
But I knew that he was wrong.
For the Sparrow said to the Robin,
"Friend I think that it must be
That they have no Heavenly Father
Such as cares for you and me".

Let us praise Him for His goodness,
Every hour of every day,
For salvation found in Jesus,
And His presence on life's way.
He has promised to be with us,
and will keep us in His care,
He has spoken words of comfort,
We must trust and never fear.

If you've never learned to trust Him,
Think of all His wondrous love,
How He gave His life to save us,
Shed for us His precious blood.
He who careth for the Sparrow,
Careth for us great and small.
Let us join the happy chorus,
"Thank you, thank you, Lord of all".

The Cost

Have you thought what it cost His Father, our God,
When His Son left the glory above?
To come to this earth away from His side
Because of the depths of His love.

Have you thought what it cost to allow Him to come
As a baby with frail, human form?
When in Bethlehem's inn, no room could be found
But a bed in a crude cattle stall.

Have you thought of the cost, as He saw His dear Son
Walking amid sin and strife?
Giving sight to the blind, making lame men to walk,
And raising death's victims to life.

Have you thought what it cost when God saw Him betrayed,
Treated with hatred and scorn?
When he stood before Pilate, despised and alone,
On His pure brow that harsh crown of thorns.

Have you thought what it cost, when to Calvary's hill
God's own, well-beloved Son was led?
When they hammered the nails in those dear healing hands
And "Father forgive them", He said.

Have you thought as He hung there between earth and heaven
How deeply His Father must care?
That men should deride and spit upon Him,
And then, sitting down, watch Him there.

Have you thought of the cost to a thrice Holy God
When the burden of sin, yours and mine,
Was laid upon Him who was sinless and pure?
Truly this was a love all divine.

Yes, the cost was tremendous, no other can know,
What He suffered to save you and me;
Bearing our judgement, forsaken of God,
That we, saved forever, might be.

Have you thought that the Father so loved you and me,
That His Son as our ransom was given?
Oh, how great was the cost, to save us, 'the lost',
That we might be with Him in Heaven.

When safe home in Glory, we see His dear face,
Those nail prints we also shall see,
They will tell of the cost, of His wonderful love,
The cost of His great love for me.

Entangled

One day I put my knitting down
Without due thought or care,
It was a foolish thing to do,
It just slipped off the chair.

A kitten got my ball of wool
And what a time he had
Up and down, and in and out,
Spinning around like mad.

The more he jumped and pranced about,
The more that tangle grew,
Around his legs and back and ears,
His tail was tangled too.

He fought so hard to free himself,
But it was all in vain,
And in the end he just gave up
Too tired to try again.

He looked at me so pleadingly,
I knew I'd have to help
To try and set that kitten free,
He could not free himself.

I got busy with the scissors
But I had to snip with care
To give that kitten freedom
And rescue him from fear.

He really was entangled
And he could plainly see
That he could never free himself
So he just trusted me.
That's what the Saviour did for us
By dying on the tree
He saved us from sin's tangles
And set out spirits free.

So as that kitten was freed at last
Through faith and trust in me
I find true rest and peace and joy
Because Christ died for me.

We are growing publishers, adding several new titles to our list each year. We also undertake private publications and commissioned works.

Our range includes:-

Books of Verse:
Devotional Poetry
Recitations for Children
Humorous Monologues

Drama
Bible Plays
Sketches
Christmas, Passiontide,
　Easter and Harvest Plays
Demonstrations

Resource Books
Assembly Material
Songs and Musicals
Children's Addresses
Prayers
Worship and Preaching
Books for Speakers

Activity Books
Quizzes
Puzzles

Church Stationery
Notice Books
Cradle Roll Certificates
Presentation Labels

Associated Lists and Imprints
Cliff College Publishing
Nimbus Press
Headway
Social Work Christian Fellowship

Please send a stamped addressed envelope (C5 approx 9" x 6") for the current catalogue or consult your local Christian Bookshop who will either stock or be able to obtain Moorleys titles.